Good News for All Nations

AN INTERNATIONAL BIBLE STUDY

MICAH COLBERT

WESTBOW
PRESS®
A DIVISION OF THOMAS NELSON
& ZONDERVAN

WestBow Press books may be ordered through booksellers or by contacting:

WestBow Press
A Division of Thomas Nelson & Zondervan
1663 Liberty Drive
Bloomington, IN 47403
www.westbowpress.com
1 (866) 928-1240

ISBN: 978-1-9736-1729-7 (sc)
ISBN: 978-1-9736-1728-0 (e)

Library of Congress Control Number: 2018901251

Print information available on the last page.

WestBow Press rev. date: 3/23/2018

CONTENTS

PREFACE

Welcome to *Good News for All Nations*. If you're looking for answers to life's big questions, or simply want to understand more about the Bible and Christianity, this study is for you.

How to Use This Handbook

Most of you will be doing this study either in a group or one-on-one with another Christian. Before each meeting, read the Bible passage for the lesson and try to answer the questions. If there's an English word that's new to you or something about the lesson you don't understand, ask your group leader for help.

If you're doing this study alone, please visit our Facebook page to connect with others who are also discovering God's good news. A link to our group can be found on our website, www. internationalbiblestudy.com.

The truths we are about to explore from God's Word will be life-changing for all who believe. Let's get started.

Your friend,

Micah Colbert

Founder, International Bible Study

INTRODUCTION

The Bible: God's Word for All People

A Brief Overview of the Bible

The Bible is unlike any other book you have ever read. It is one book made up of sixty-six distinct books. It was written by more than forty authors over a fifteen hundred–year period. The Bible, however, isn't just a collection of different people's stories or opinions about God. Unlike other religious books written by people, the Bible is the Word of God.

The Bible is divided into two main parts: the Old Testament (thirty-nine books) and the New Testament (twenty-seven books). The Old Testament tells us about the times before Jesus. The New Testament focuses on the life and teachings of Jesus, as well as the spread of Christianity. Each book of the Bible has

My Notes

chapters and verses so that we can remember where things are found.

The Bible Is God's Word

"Your word is truth; and every one of your righteous [perfect] rules endures forever." (Psalm 119:160)

"All Scripture [the words of the Bible] is breathed out by God." (2 Timothy 3:16)

"For **prophecy** never had its **origin** in the human will [it didn't come from people], but **prophets**, though human, spoke from God as they were carried along by the Holy Spirit." (2 Peter 1:20–21 NIV)

These verses teach us that the words of the Bible were "breathed out" or given to us by God. The authors didn't write their own ideas, but were specially guided by God to write His exact words. The Bible's **unity**, **accuracy**, consistency, fulfilled prophecies, historical truthfulness, and message all show us that the Bible is God's Word.

Because the Bible is God's Word, it should be the authority in our lives. If we want to know what to believe or how to live, we can look to the Bible as our God-given, perfect, and trustworthy guide.

The Bible: Good News for All People

God has given us His Word so that we might know Him. The Bible shows us who God is and teaches us how we can have a relationship with Him.

To know God, we need to know the good news about Jesus. The Bible calls this good news the *gospel*. The main story of the Bible— the one message that unites all the books, chapters, and verses together—focuses on the life, death, and **resurrection** of Jesus.

This is the story we will be exploring over the next few weeks through our study.

Conclusion: Discussion Questions

- What makes the Bible different from other religious books?
- Why was the Bible written?
- Do you think the Bible is important? If so, why?
- How would your life change if you believe the Bible is God's Word?

ESL Words and Meanings

- **Made up**: To combine two or more things together to make something new or larger. "Made up" is a common phrasal verb. Phrasal verbs are two words (a verb and a preposition) that are combined to make one new word.
- **Prophecy**: Something said in the past about the future that became true.
- **Origin**: Beginning; where something comes from.
- **Prophets**: Those who received a message from God to tell other people.
- **Unity**: All the words and books of the Bible are in perfect agreement with each other. They never contradict or disagree with one another.
- **Accuracy**: Free from mistakes or errors.
- **Gospel**: The good news of how God brings sinful people into a relationship with Himself through Jesus. This good news is what we will be exploring throughout our lessons.
- **Resurrection**: To come to life again.

God: The Creator and King

Introduction

Who am I? Why am I here? What's my purpose in life? These are some of the questions people all over the world have been asking for centuries. Thankfully, we don't have to **figure out** what life is about on our own. God's Word gives us the answers in a true story we call the gospel (see previous lesson).

We begin our study of this story where God begins: in the first chapters in the first book of the Bible.

Bible Reading: Genesis 1, 2:15–25.

My Notes

General Questions

- What is happening in this passage?
- What does this passage teach us about God?
- What does this passage teach us about people?
- What does this passage teach us about the relationship between God and people?

Specific Questions

- Is everything the result of **chance**, or was the world made specifically by God?
- What happens when people don't believe there is a God who made everything?
- How did God create "the heavens and the earth"?
- According to Genesis 1:26–27, what makes people different from the rest of God's creation?
- What did God command Adam to do in Genesis 2:16–17? What would happen if Adam did not believe God or obey His command?

Important Explanations

In the beginning, God created: Before the world began, God was there. Psalm 90:2 says, "Even from everlasting to everlasting [forever], you are God." The God who needed nothing made everything. Because He made all things, He alone has the right to rule over all things.

Made in God's image: In some ways, we are like God. Like God, we have a mind, **will**, and emotions. We have a **soul** that will live forever. We have a sense of what is right and wrong. Because we are made in God's image, we can have a personal relationship with God and with one another.

Additional Reading

"O Lord [King], you are **worthy** to receive glory and honor and power, because You created all things, and for **Your will** they are and were created." (Revelation 4:11 NIV)

- Why did God make everything? Why did God make you?

Conclusion

The world did not begin by **chance**. The almighty God made the heavens and the earth. On the final day of creation, He made the first man and woman, Adam and Eve. God made us in His image so that we would **glorify** Him and enjoy a relationship with Him. John 17:3 calls this relationship "eternal life." On the final day of creation, God said that everything He made was good. Everything was exactly the way God planned it to be.

For Further Study

To learn more about what God is like, please read the appendix article at the end of this handbook.

ESL Words and Meanings

- **Figure out**: To understand something or to solve a problem.
- **Chance**: Something that happens that seems to have no purpose or reason.
- **Will**: We can make choices and decisions.
- **Soul**: The words *soul* and *spirit* are used in the Bible to refer to the eternal part of us. When Adam was created, he was given a body, but he wasn't considered alive until God "breathed into his nostrils the breath of life, and ... [he] became a living soul" (see Genesis 2:7). Our bodies will one day die, but our souls will live somewhere forever. We will either experience life forever with God or death forever apart from God.
- **Worthy**: God deserves to be admired, loved, and praised by everyone because He made all things.
- **Your will**: God's purpose. Because God made all things for His will, our lives have purpose.
- **Glorify**: To honor God by 1) seeing and loving God's greatness and 2) helping others see how great God is.

Man: The Rebellious Sinner

Introduction

In our first lesson, we learned that God made everything. He made people in His image so that we could have a personal relationship with Him. God placed the first man and woman, Adam and Eve, in a beautiful garden where they lived in perfect harmony with God and with one another. They were free to enjoy all of God's good creation. There was only one thing they couldn't do: eat from the tree of the knowledge of good and evil (see Genesis 2:16–17). God gave them this command as a test. Would they believe in God's goodness and obey Him as King, or would they **rebel** against Him?

My Notes

Bible Reading: Genesis 3:1–24; Romans 5:12.

General Questions

- What is happening in this passage?
- What does this passage teach us about God?
- What does this passage teach us about people?
- What does this passage teach us about the relationship between God and people?

Specific Questions

Verses 1–7

- How did the serpent **tempt** Eve? What did he tell her?
- Why did Eve eat the fruit? Why did Adam eat the fruit?
- What happened after Adam and Eve disobeyed God (see verse 7)?

Verses 10–13

- Why were Adam and Eve afraid?
- What did Adam and Eve do when God questioned them?

Verses 15, 23–25

- What did God promise Adam and Eve?
- What happened because of Adam and Eve's disobedience?
- In what way did Adam and Eve die after they disobeyed?

Important Explanations

Serpent: Revelation 12:9 and 20:2 tell us that the serpent (or snake) was Satan. Satan is a powerful angel created by God who chose to **rebel** against God as King. Satan wants to **deceive** people into believing his lies so that they do not believe God or obey Him.

Die/Death: Death is separation. The Bible mentions three kinds of death: physical, spiritual, and eternal (forever) death. The death Adam, Eve, and the rest of humanity experienced was spiritual—separation from a forever relationship with God.

Genesis 3:15: God promised that He would send a **Savior** who would crush Satan and defeat his plan to lead everyone into **sin**, **rebellion**, and **eternal destruction**. This Savior would come from the woman (her "seed") and make a way for people to have life with God once again.

ESL Words and Meanings

- **Rebel/rebellion**: To oppose or disobey someone; to refuse to obey a leader.
- **Tempt**: To make a person want to do or have something that isn't good.
- **Deceive**: To try to make someone believe a lie.
- **Savior**: The one who rescues people from sin and its judgment (spiritual and eternal death).
- **Sin**: To rebel against God's authority. Sin refers not only to actions but even words, thoughts, and attitudes that break God's commands.
- **Eternal destruction**: Another way of talking about eternal death; separation from God in a place of punishment called hell (see Matthew 13:42; 25:41, 46; etc.).

Conclusion

Instead of trusting God and obeying Him as King, Adam and Eve chose to believe Satan's lie and rebel against God. Through their rebellion, sin and death entered the world. The perfect relationship humanity enjoyed with God was now dead. God removed Adam and Eve from the garden but gave them a promise of good news. One of their descendants (children) would defeat Satan's plan, rescue people from sin, and bring people back into harmony with God again.

Sin: The Rebellion Spreads

Introduction

If God is good, then why is there so much evil and suffering in the world? Why is there so much injustice, pain, corruption, and death? Everywhere we look, we see the effects of sin. Is there any hope that things can be made right?

Bible Reading: Genesis 4:1–12, 6:1–8.

General Questions

- What is happening in this passage?
- What does this passage teach us about God?
- What does this passage teach us about people?

My Notes

- What does this passage teach us about the relationship between God and people?

Specific Questions

- Why did God accept Abel's sacrifice (see Hebrews 11:4 below)?
- Why didn't God accept Cain's sacrifice?
- Why was Cain angry?
- What did Cain do to his brother Abel?
- Do you think Genesis 6:5 describes people's hearts today? Does this verse describe your heart?

Additional Verses

"Sin entered the world through one man, and death through sin, and in this way death came to all people, because all sinned." (Romans 5:12 NIV)

"All we like sheep have gone astray; we have turned—every one—to his own way." (Isaiah 53:6)

"The heart is **deceitful** above all things, and desperately sick: who can understand it?" (Jeremiah 17:9)

"By faith Abel brought God a better offering than Cain did. By faith he was **commended** as righteous when God spoke well of his offerings." (Hebrews 11:4 NIV)

Important Explanations

Sin: Sin is rebellion against God's authority as King. Sin refers not only to actions, but even words, thoughts, attitudes, and **motives** that break God's commands. Not only do we commit acts of sin (Romans 3:23), but our hearts are sinful as well (Jeremiah 17:9).

Heart: The heart refers to who we are on the inside. The heart consists of our mind, will, and emotions. When Genesis 6:5 said that people's hearts were "evil continually," it meant that everything about them (what they thought, the emotions they felt, and the things they did) was sinful.

Cain's offering: Cain's sacrifice was rejected because he did not offer it by faith. He did not believe or obey God because of the sin in his own heart.

Faith: Faith is a trust, dependence, or belief in God that results in obedience to God. Unlike Cain, Abel believed God and received grace – favor or blessing from God that cannot be earned (see Ephesians 2:8-9). The grace we all need to have a right relationship with God is received through faith.

Righteous (Hebrews 11:4): God **commended** Abel as righteous because Abel believed God and trusted in His Word. When God says that someone is righteous, He is not saying that the person is perfect or has no sin. Rather, He is saying that the person's sins are forgiven so that they are no longer spiritually dead (separated from God). Through faith, they are made right with God.

Conclusion

Through Adam's rebellion, sin and death came into the world and spread to all people. Instead of obeying God, we have chosen to live in rebellion against Him. Even though Cain and Abel were both born with sinful hearts, God considered Abel "righteous." Hebrews 11:4 tells us that he was righteous because he believed God and trusted in His Word. Through faith, Abel received God's grace. He was forgiven and brought into a relationship with God.

ESL WORDS AND MEANINGS

- **Deceitful**: To tell lies. The heart lies to us by telling us we're okay and that our sin is not that bad.
- **Commended**: To speak or think highly of someone because of something they've done.
- **Motives**: The reasons for our actions (why we do what we do).

Separation: Sin Keeps Us from God

Introduction

We have learned that God made us in His image so that we could enjoy a relationship with Him. Because of sin, this relationship has been broken. Sin has affected all of us. We are all "dead in sin" (Ephesians 2:1), separated from life with God.

Bible Reading: Exodus 20:1–17.

General Questions

- What is happening in this passage?
- What does this passage teach us about God?
- What does this passage teach us about people?
- What does this passage teach us about the relationship between God and people?

My Notes

Important Explanations

There are two problems that keep us from a relationship with God.

Problem 1: We Have Broken God's Law

The Ten Commandments found in Exodus 20 help us understand how **holy** God is. By looking at these rules, we quickly realize that we are not **holy**. We are **sinners** who are **guilty** of breaking God's law. For example:

- *Do Not Lie*: Lying is not telling the full truth. We lie when we deceive others by making them believe something that isn't true. Because God is always truthful, He hates lies and will punish those who lie.

- *Do Not Covet*: Coveting is strongly wanting something that isn't ours. We covet because we are not happy with what we have. We might covet someone's things, money, job, possessions, etc.

- *Do Not Commit Adultery*: Jesus tells us in Matthew 5:27–28 that people who **lust** commit adultery in their hearts. Anyone who has sex outside of marriage is also guilty of breaking this command.

- *Love God with All Your Heart*: We break God's rules because we love ourselves more than God. Our hearts are naturally selfish, focused more on pleasing ourselves than God.

Some might say, "But I'm a nice person. I may have broken a few of God's laws, but I try to live a good life. Compared to others, I'm not that bad."

Read the following verses and answer the questions below.

"All of us have become like one who is unclean, and all our righteous acts [good works] are like filthy rags." (Isaiah 64:6 NIV)

"Surely there is not a righteous [perfect] man on earth who does good and never sins." (Ecclesiastes 7:20)

"For whoever keeps the whole law but fails in one point has become guilty of [breaking] all of it." (James 2:10)

- According to the Bible, are there any good people?
- What does God say our good works are like?
- How many laws can a person break before he or she becomes guilty of breaking the whole law?

Sin makes us **guilty** before God. There's nothing we can do to make ourselves clean from sin. The good things we do, compared to how holy God is, are like dirty rags. They have no power to make us **righteous**.

We might think that we're good people, but we're not. We have broken God's law. The law is like a chain. If one link is broken, the whole chain is destroyed. God's Word is clear: because of sin, we cannot be **righteous** before God through good works (see also Galatians 2:16; Romans 3:20).

Problem 2: We Have Sinful Hearts

Read the following verses and answer the questions below.

"For from within, out of the heart of man, come evil thoughts, sexual immorality, theft, murder, adultery ... All these evil things come from within, and they **defile** a person." (Mark 7:20–23)

"The heart is deceitful above all things and desperately sick; who can understand it?" (Jeremiah 17:9)

- Where does sin come from?
- How does the Bible describe our hearts?

Sin has changed our hearts. By **nature**, we are sinful. Think about it ... did anyone teach us how to be selfish, how to get angry with other people, or lie? Of course not! We do these things because we are born with sinful hearts that **naturally** rebel against God. Sin has affected everything about us. Sin makes it impossible for us to earn a relationship with a holy God. We cannot save ourselves from sin and its punishment.

The Consequence of Sin: Death

Read the following verses, and answer the questions below.

"For the **wages** of sin is death." (Romans 6:23)

"But your iniquities [sins] have made a separation between you and your God, and your sins have hidden His face from you, so that He does not hear." (Isaiah 59:2)

- What have we earned for our sin?
- What separates people from God?

Because God is holy, He must judge sin. The punishment of sin is death, separation from God both in this life and forever. Eternal death is also referred to as hell in the Bible.

The Bible describes hell as a real place where real people experience punishment for their sin forever (see Matthew 13:42, 25:41; Mark 9:43; Jude 1:7; Revelation 21:8).

Someone might say, "But how could a good God send anyone to hell?" God is loving, but God is also a holy Judge. He will punish those who have broken His law because He hates sin. Our sin is so serious that the only fair punishment for sin is eternal death.

Conclusion

There's nothing we can do to change our sinful hearts or take away our sinful actions. We are guilty before God and deserve God's judgment. But God is a God of love. In our next lessons, we will look at the good news of what God has done for us so that we can be forgiven and have a relationship with Him.

ESL Words and Meanings

- **Holy**: God is absolutely perfect and separated from all that is sinful.
- **Sinners**: People who sin. We are all sinners because we are born with sinful hearts that naturally rebel against God.
- **Guilty**: Responsible for sin and wrongdoing.
- **Content**: To be happy or satisfied.
- **Lust**: Looking at someone who is not your wife or husband with sexual desire.
- **Righteous**: To be in a right relationship with God.
- **Defile**: To make dirty. Sin makes us unclean or impure in the sight of a holy God.
- **Nature/naturally**: To describe something that happens by itself without being controlled or changed by someone else.
- **Wages**: What someone earns for his or her work. Because of sin, we all deserve eternal death.

TRANSITION

In the first four lessons, we have learned the following:

- The world is not here by chance. God made everything. Because He is the Creator, He is King or Lord over His creation.
- God made us in His image so that we could have a relationship with Him. God calls this relationship "eternal life" (John 17:3).
- Instead of believing God and obeying Him, we have chosen to rebel against God. Because of sin, our relationship with God is dead. We are born with sinful hearts and reject God's rule over our lives.
- God shows us how holy He is through His law. We have all broken His law and deserve judgment. The judgment of sin is death—separation from God both now and forever in hell.
- There is nothing we can do on our own to change our sinful hearts or earn a relationship with God.

If the story of the Bible stopped here, we wouldn't call it good news. But it doesn't. Thankfully, there's hope.

LESSON 5

Jesus: God's Promised Savior

Introduction

Before God removed Adam and Eve from the garden, He made them (and us) a promise. God said that He would send a Savior—someone who would save people from sin and its punishment. The story of the Old Testament is an incredible story of how God prepared the way for this promised Savior. But who would this person be?

Jesus's Miraculous Birth

Read the verses and answer the questions below:

"This is how the birth of Jesus the Messiah [the promised Savior] came about: His mother Mary was pledged [promised] to be married to Joseph, but

My Notes

before they came together, she was found to be pregnant through the Holy Spirit. Because Joseph her husband was faithful to the law, and he did not want to expose her to public disgrace, he had in mind to divorce her quietly. But after he had considered this, an angel of the Lord appeared to him in a dream and said, 'Joseph son of David, do not be afraid to take Mary home as your wife, because what is conceived in her is from the Holy Spirit. She will give birth to a son, and you are to give him the name Jesus, because he will save his people from their sins.' All this took place to fulfill what the Lord had said through the **prophet**: 'The virgin will conceive and give birth to a son, and they will call him Immanuel' (which means 'God with us').' When Joseph woke up, he did what the angel of the Lord had commanded him and took Mary home as his wife. But he did not consummate their marriage until she gave birth to a son. And he gave him the name Jesus." (Matthew 1:18–25 NIV)

"And the angel said to them, 'Fear not, for behold, I bring you good news of great joy that will be for all the people. For unto you is born this day in the city of David a Savior, who is Christ the Lord.'" (Luke 2:10–11)

- Who is the promised Savior?
- What makes Jesus's birth such a **miracle**?
- How did Jesus's birth fulfill **prophecy**?
- Why did the angel tell Joseph to name the baby Jesus?
- What would Jesus save people from?
- Why was the coming of Jesus considered "good news of great joy"?
- What do these verses tell us about Jesus?

There is a lot of confusion today about who Jesus is. Many people say that He's just a prophet, teacher, religious leader, or good man. But the Bible makes it clear that Jesus is unlike anyone else in history. Jesus is Immanuel, God with us. He is the Savior God promised to Adam, Eve, and all humanity. He is the one who came to rescue people from sin and bring them back to God.

Fully God, Fully Man

Read the verses and answer the questions below:

"In the beginning was the Word, and the Word was with God, and the Word was God. All things were made through him, and without him was not anything made that was made... and the Word became flesh and dwelt [lived] among us. And we have seen His glory, glory as of the only Son from the Father." (John 1:1,3,14)

"And we know that the Son of God has come and has given us understanding, so that we may know him who is true; and we are in him who is true, in his Son Jesus Christ. He is the true God and eternal life." (1 John 5:20)

- Who is the Word?
- Who made the world?
- What did the Word become?
- What does the last sentence of 1 John 5:20 tell us about Jesus?

Jesus is not just a good man or religious teacher. He's God! The God who made all things became a man so that we could know Him. Hebrews 4:15 tells us that Jesus experienced the same struggles, difficulties, and troubles that we do, yet did so without sin. Jesus, fully God and fully man, is the Savior we need to bring us to God.

The Mediator between God and Man

"For there is one God and one mediator between God and men [people], the man Christ Jesus." (1 Timothy 2:5)

A mediator is someone who **restores** a broken relationship between two people. Because of sin, our relationship with God is broken. We can't make this relationship right again because we are sinners who have broken God's law. But Jesus isn't a sinner. He's God! Only Jesus, the perfect Savior, can bring sinful people into a relationship with a holy God.

Important Explanations

Jesus the Messiah: The word Messiah means "chosen one." Jesus is the Messiah that the **prophets** said would come (see John 4:25–26). He is the one God chose to save people from their sin.

A Savior, who is Christ the Lord: This phrase tells us a lot about who Jesus is. First, He is a Savior. He rescues people from sin and its punishment. He is also the Christ, the promised Deliver who would bring people back to God again. Finally, He is Lord. He is the great King over all creation.

The Word: This is a title for Jesus. As the Word, Jesus shows us exactly what God is like.

The Word became flesh: Jesus, who is the eternal God, became a man. When He became a man, He did not stop being God. He was fully God and fully man at the same time (but without sin).

He is the true God and eternal life: God's Word makes it clear that Jesus is not just another man. He is God. He became a man so that He could be the Savior we need to bring us to God. Through Jesus we can have eternal life.

Conclusion

Jesus is God's promised Savior. His **miraculous** birth fulfilled the **prophecies** in the Old Testament about God sending a Savior. Being fully God and perfect man, Jesus has the power to save us from sin. What He did to save us is what we will discover in our next lesson.

ESL Words and Meanings

- **Miracle/miraculous**: Something that is so supernatural that it cannot be explained by science.
- **Prophet**: Someone who received a message from God to tell other people.
- **Prophecies**: Something said in the past about the future that became true. Most of the Bible's prophecies are about Jesus. Hundreds of years before Jesus came, prophets predicted exact details about how and where Jesus would be born (Isaiah 7:14, Micah 5:2), live (Isaiah 9:6–7), and die (Isaiah 53).
- **Restore**: to repair or put back together again.

Jesus: The Way to God

Introduction

My Notes

Because God is holy and **just**, He must punish sin. But God is love. In His love, God provided a way for guilty sinners to be made right with Him.

"But God shows His love for us in that while we were still sinners, Christ died for us." (Romans 5:12)

"For Christ also suffered [died] once for sins, the righteous [perfect] for the unrighteous [sinners], that He might bring us to God." (1 Peter 3:18)

- How does God show sinners His love?
- Who did Jesus die for?
- Why did Jesus die?

Jesus in My Place

Read the verses and answer the questions.

"The wages [payment or punishment] of sin is death." (Romans 6:23a)

"Christ died *for our sins* in accordance with the **Scriptures**, that he was buried, that he was raised on the third day in accordance with the **Scriptures**." (1 Corinthians 15:3–4)

- Why did Jesus die?
- Why would Jesus have to die for our sins?

In His love, Jesus did for us what we could not do for ourselves. We can't keep the law. He did. We are not perfect or good. He is. We deserve death for our sin. He died in the place of all who would believe in Him. Because Jesus died as a **substitute**, we can be forgiven and know the joy of having eternal life with God. The good news of God's Word can be summarized in these four words: "Jesus in my place."

The Risen Savior

"He is not here, for he has risen, as he said. Come, see the place where he lay." (Matthew 28:6)

"Christ has been raised from the dead... For as by a man [Adam] came death, by a man [Jesus] has come also the resurrection of the dead [life forever with God]." (1 Corinthians 15:20–21)

The resurrection of Jesus is the most important event in human history. It proves that Jesus is who He said He is: the one true God who is King over all the earth. The resurrection demonstrated that Jesus's **sacrifice** was accepted by God as a payment for sin's punishment (death). Because Jesus is alive, those who trust in Him can also experience life forever with God.

The Only Way to God

Look up the following verses and answer the questions.

"I am the door. If anyone enters by Me, he will be saved [from sin]... I am the way, the truth, and the life. No one comes to the Father [God] except through Me [Jesus]." (John 10:9, 14:6)

- Can a person come to God any way he or she wants?
- How many ways can a person come to God?
- How can a person be made right with God?

Jesus is the only way to God. There is no other way. He kept God's law and lived the perfect life we cannot. He died so that we wouldn't have to be separated from God. He rose again so that we might have eternal life. Through Him we can be forgiven and made right with God.

Important Explanations

God shows His love: God's love is very different than the "love" we often hear about today. God doesn't love people because they are good, attractive, or lovely. He loves because He is love. He demonstrated His never-ending love by sending His Son, Jesus, to take away sin's death penalty for those who would trust in Him.

Died for our sins: The punishment of sin is death (Romans 6:23). We deserve to die forever because of our sin. Jesus died so that those who believe in Him could be rescued from sin and death. Because of Jesus, sinners who deserve to die can be forgiven and have life forever with God.

Conclusion

What great news! Everything we need to be saved from sin is provided for us through Jesus. He alone is the one who can bring us to God. The good news of what Jesus has done, however, demands a response.

ESL Words and Meanings

- **Scriptures**: Another term that refers to the Bible. The word *Scriptures* means "holy writings."
- **Just**: Morally right or good. God is a God of justice, always doing what is right. He cannot ignore sin because His law has been broken.
- **Substitute**: Someone who does something in place of another. Jesus perfectly kept God's law and died in our place to fully pay sin's penalty (death) for us.
- **Sacrifice**: To die in the place of someone else as a payment for his or her sin. Only Jesus could die in the place of sinful people because He is sinless.
- **Resurrection**: To come back to life again.

Responding to Jesus: Turn and Trust

Introduction

Everything we need to be rescued from sin and made right with God is available to us through Jesus. Jesus, God's promised Savior, died so that we don't have to be separated from God forever. He rose again to prove that He is God. The good news of everything Jesus has done demands a response.

Rescued by Grace

Read the verses and answer the questions below:

"For by grace you have been saved through faith. And this is not your own doing; it is the

My Notes

gift of God, not a result of works, so that no one may boast [be proud]." (Ephesians 2:8–9)

"For the wages [payment] of sin is death, but the free gift of God is eternal life in Christ Jesus our Lord." (Romans 6:23)

- How are people saved from sin and its penalty?
- Why can't people be saved from sin by their own works?
- Is eternal life—a forever relationship with God—a gift or a reward?

Grace is God freely giving sinners like you and me something we don't deserve and could never earn. It is through God's grace that we can have **salvation** from sin and life forever with Him.

Unlike the false "gods" of the nations who must be **appeased** through rituals, offerings, and religious performances, the God of the Bible is a God of grace. He is a Savior.

We could never come to God because of sin, so God came to us. He sent His Son to live the perfect life we couldn't and die the death we deserve so that we could experience the joy of God's grace. So how does this grace become ours?

Receiving Grace: Turning and Trusting

Read the verses and answer the questions below:

"Repent and believe the **gospel**." (Mark 1:15)

"[God] commands all people everywhere to repent." (Acts 17:30)

"For God so loved the world, that he gave his only Son [Jesus], that whoever believes in him should not perish [experience death forever in hell] but have eternal life." (John 3:16)

"Believe in the Lord Jesus, and you will be saved [from sin]." (Acts 16:31)

- What does God command all people to do?
- What will happen to the person who truly believes in Jesus?

To receive God's grace, we must repent and believe.

Important Explanations

1. Repent/Repentance

To repent means to turn *from* sin *to* God *through* faith in Jesus. When people repent, the following things happen:

- They admit that they are sinners who deserve to die forever because of their sin.
- They hate their sin and have no desire to continue living in rebellion against God.
- They know that there is nothing they can do on their own to take away sin's punishment
- They turn to God, trusting only in His grace to receive forgiveness and eternal life.

Sadly, many people love their sin so much that they would rather have sin than God. They would rather hold on to their rebellion than turn to God through faith in Christ. We must not let love for sin, self, and the things of this world keep us from turning to the Lord.

People can only repent as they turn to God through faith (or belief) in Jesus.

2. Believe/Faith

Faith is completely depending upon Jesus alone for forgiveness from sin and eternal life. When people trust in Jesus for a forever relationship with God, the following things happen.

- They believe what the Bible says about God, people, and Jesus is true.
- They believe that only Jesus can forgive them and bring them to God
- They stop trusting in their good works to save themselves from sin. Instead, they place their trust and hope in Jesus's death and resurrection as the only way of being made right with God.

What Happens If I Repent and Believe?

Read the verse and answer the questions below:

"To all who did receive him [Jesus], to those who believed in his name, he [God] gave the right to become children of God." (John 1:12)

"Whoever believes in the Son [Jesus] has eternal life; whoever does not obey the Son shall not see life, but the wrath of God remains on him." (John 3:36)

"Truly, truly, I say to you, whoever hears my [Jesus's] word and believes him who sent me has eternal life. He does not come into judgment [for sin], but has passed from death to life." (John 5:24)

"I [Jesus] give them [those who believe in Jesus] eternal life, and they will never perish, and no one will snatch [take] them out of my hand." (John 10:28)

- What happens to all who receive Jesus?
- What will happen to those who don't obey Jesus's command to repent and believe?
- Is it possible for those who truly believe in Jesus to experience eternal death?
- Who has eternal life? Will those who have eternal life ever perish (die forever)?

These verses show us that those who repent and trust in Jesus pass from death to life, become God's children, have a forever relationship with God, and never experience sin's judgment. All these amazing gifts of grace are available to anyone who will turn from sin and trust in Jesus.

Conclusion

The truths we have studied from God's Word demand a response. We will either reject Jesus or trust in Him. We will either continue in rebellion against God or turn to Him in repentance and faith. We cannot remain **neutral**. We must decide.

"Now is the accepted time; behold, now is the day of **salvation**." (2 Corinthians 6:2)

ESL Words and Meanings

- **Salvation**: To be saved, rescued, or delivered from sin and its penalty.
- **Appeased**: To satisfy or try to gain someone's favor.
- **Gospel**: The good news of how God brings sinful people into a relationship with Himself through Jesus.
- **Neutral**: Undecided. Not committed to either option.

CONCLUSION

If you have any questions or would like to further research what you've studied from God's Word, please visit our website at www. internationalbiblestudy.com. On our site, you will find videos, articles, and resources that will help you grow in your understanding of God's Word. If you repent and believe in Jesus, we would love to know about it! We would love to help you take the next steps in your new relationship with God. We look forward to hearing from you soon.

God in Three Persons: The Triune God of the Bible

By: Dr. Matthew Conrad

Introduction

The one true God is a God who is very hard to describe! Human words cannot completely explain who God is and what He is like. In the Bible, God tells us about Himself. God made everything, but God Himself was not made. He is eternal, which means He has no beginning or end. There is no god like the one true God. One way God is completely unique is in His triunity. What is the trinity or God's triunity? These words mean that God is one God who exists as three persons. Let's see what God says in the Bible.

One God

The Bible clearly teaches that there is only one true God (see Deuteronomy 6:4; Exodus 20:2–3; Psalm 86:10; 1 Corinthians 8:4; Ephesians 4:3–6; James 2:19; 1 Timothy 2:5; etc.).

"Hear, O Israel: The Lord our God, the Lord is one." (Deuteronomy 6:4)

"I am the LORD, and there is no other, besides me there is no God." (Isaiah 45:5)

Three Persons

Clearly, there is only one God, but the Bible speaks of three persons who are God. These three persons are God the Father, God the Son, and God the Holy Spirit.

    1.   God the Father is God.

"One God and Father of all, who is above all, and through all, and in all." (Ephesians 4:6)

"Grace to you and peace from God our Father and the Lord Jesus Christ." (Romans 1:7)

    2.   God the Son is God.

Jesus Christ is God the Son (John 1:1–14; Isaiah 9:6; Hebrews 1:8; John 10:30; 1 John 5:20; Titus 2:13). God became man. Jesus had names that only belonged to God. He had attributes or characteristics that only God has. Jesus did miracles that only God can do. He accepted worship as God that only God should accept (Matthew 14:33; 28:9–10; John 9:37–38; Hebrews 1:6). Jesus publicly claimed He was one with God (John 10:30, 17:21). The Bible says Jesus is equal with God (Philippians 2:6). Finally, Jesus rose from the dead, proving He is God (1 Corinthians 15).

"I and my Father are one." (John 10:30)

"In the beginning was the Word [Jesus Christ], and the Word was with God, and the Word was God ... And the Word [Jesus Christ] became flesh and dwelt among us, and we have seen His glory, the glory as of the only Son from the Father, full of grace and truth." (John 1:1, 14)

3. "God the Holy Spirit is God." (Acts 5:3–4, 28:25–27; 2 Corinthians 3:17)

"But Peter said, 'Ananias, why has Satan filled your heart to lie to the Holy Spirit ... You have not lied to man but to God.'" (Acts 5:3–4)

These Three Persons Are One God

Even though the Father, Son, and Holy Spirit are three distinct persons, God is one unified God. Many verses in the Bible teach this truth and show the Father, Son, and Holy Spirit as one working together in unity (Genesis 1:26–27; Matthew 3:16–17, 28:19; Luke 1:35, 24:49; John 14:16–17a; Romans 15:16; 2 Corinthians 1:21–22, 13:14; Galatians 4:6; Ephesians 3:14–19; 2 Thessalonians 2:13–14; Hebrews 9:14; 1 Peter 1:1–2; 1 John 5:7; Jude 20–21).

"Go therefore and make disciples of all the nations, baptizing them in the name of the Father and of the Son and of the Holy Spirit." (Matthew 28:19)

"The grace of the Lord Jesus Christ and the love of God and the fellowship of the Holy Spirit be with you all. Amen." (2 Corinthians 13:14)

No Other God Is Like the God of the Bible

The trinity (this truth about God being one God in three persons) is unique to the Bible. The gods of Islam, Buddhism, Hinduism, and other non-Christian religions are very different from the one true God of the Bible.

- The god of Islam is Allah. Islam teaches that their god is one god, but it does not teach that their god exists as three persons. The Koran teaches that Allah is god and that Jesus is just a human prophet.

- The first principles or ultimate realities of Buddhism are not the same as the God of the Bible. God is a spirit. Everything came from Him and will return to Him. However, God also became man to save human beings from sin, which is the real cause of their suffering. True enlightenment does not come from inside a person. It does not come through following a path of teaching. True enlightenment can only come from the one true God. He knows everything because He made everything. Through the Bible, God reveals His knowledge to human beings.

- Hinduism teaches that there are many gods with different qualities and abilities, not one almighty God in three persons.

Summary

As you can see, the Bible teaches that God is one being with three distinct, eternal, coequal persons. In other words, there is only one God, and this one God exists in three persons. The Father is not the Son. The Son is not the Holy Spirit. The Holy Spirit is not the Father. Each person is distinct, yet each is equally and completely God. This truth is hard for our minds to understand and difficult for us to explain. God is greater than we are. We cannot totally understand everything about Him, but we can believe what God says about Himself.

Dr. Matthew Conrad is missionary church planter and Bible teacher in East Asia.

A B O U T   T H E   A U T H O R

Micah Colbert (M.Div and M.S.Ed in TESOL) has been working with international students as an ESL teacher and pastor for more than 10 years. Currently, Micah serves as the lead pastor of a multi-cultural church in Buffalo, NY. He and his wife, Debbie, live in the Buffalo area with their three children.

Printed in the United States
By Bookmasters